SERIAL KILLERS

Harold Shipman

Dr. Death

by Carla Mooney

Essential Library
An Imprint of Abdo Publishing
abdobooks.com

ABDOBOOKS.COM

Published by Abdo Publishing, a division of ABDO, PO Box 398166, Minneapolis, Minnesota 55439.

Printed in China.
102024
012025

THIS BOOK CONTAINS RECYCLED MATERIALS

Cover Photo: Greater Manchester Police/Getty Images News/Getty Images
Interior Photos: Nigel Dickinson/Shutterstock Images, 4–5; Phil Noble/PA Images/Getty Images, 6, 71, 78–79, 86; Kevin Holt/Daily Mail/Shutterstock Images, 9, 48, 51; Shutterstock Images, 13, 72; Universal History Archive/Universal Images Group/Getty Images, 14–15; Dennis Hussey/Daily Mirror/Mirrorpix/Getty Images, 20; Mirrorpix/Getty Images, 24–25; MEN Media, 28, 39; Paul White 1990s Britain/Alamy, 31; Mirrorpix, 32, 36–37, 46–47, 66–67; PA Images/Getty Images, 43, 61, 82; David Kendall/PA Images/Getty Images, 52; The Sun/News Licensing, 56–57; PA Images/Alamy, 59; Reuters/Bridgeman Images, 68; Mark Waugh/Alamy, 76; Julia Quenzler/PAMPC PA/AP Images, 85; Phil Noble/AFP/Getty Images, 90–91; A.P.S. (UK)/Alamy, 92; Martin Rickett/PA Images/Getty Images, 94

Editor: Christa Kelly
Series Designer: Joshua Olson

Library of Congress Control Number: 2024938305

PUBLISHER'S CATALOGING-IN-PUBLICATION DATA

Names: Mooney, Carla, author.
Title: Harold Shipman: Dr. Death / by Carla Mooney
Other title: Dr. Death
Description: Minneapolis, Minnesota: ABDO Publishing, 2025 | Series: Serial killers | Includes online resources and index.
Identifiers: ISBN 9781098295349 (lib. bdg.) | ISBN 9798384916345 (ebook)
Subjects: LCSH: Shipman, Harold Frederick, 1946-2004--Juvenile literature. | Death, Dr., 1946-2004--Juvenile literature. | Killers (Murderers)--Biographies--Juvenile literature. | Serial killers--Biographies--Juvenile literature. | Crime--Juvenile literature. | True crime stories--Juvenile literature.
Classification: DDC 364.15232--dc23

CONTENTS

This book discusses accounts of crime, violence, and death that may be disturbing to some readers.

CHAPTER 1

UNEARTHING A MURDER

On August 1, 1998, rain poured from a black, moonless sky as the police entered a cemetery in Hyde, a town in Greater Manchester, England. It was early morning, and the police had an unpleasant task ahead of them. They had been sent to dig up the coffin of Kathleen Grundy, an 81-year-old woman who had died five weeks earlier.

Grundy was a respected member of the community and the former mayor of Hyde. Even at age 81, she had been active and volunteered for several local charities.

Kathleen Grundy was buried in Hyde Cemetery in Hyde, England.

BAINES
MORIALS
39 - 2

Angela Woodruff was the only child of Kathleen and John Grundy.

Her death had been a shock to her friends and family, including her daughter, Angela Woodruff.

A few weeks after her mother's death, Woodruff's grief turned to suspicion. A poorly written will surfaced in which Grundy inexplicably left her entire estate to her doctor, Harold Shipman. After making a few inquiries, Woodruff went to the police and told them she believed the will had been forged.

When the police looked at the copy of the will, they agreed with Woodruff. It was apparent they were dealing with a forgery and fraud case. For Detective Inspector

Stan Egerton with the Greater Manchester Police, the main suspect was clear: the doctor who benefited from Grundy's will.

Harold Shipman was a well-known, popular doctor with a thriving medical practice. It was hard to imagine that he would forge a patient's will. But then Egerton remembered another investigation earlier that year involving Shipman. The doctor had been reported to police because of the large number of deaths among his patients. Woodruff had said that her mother's death was unexpected. Now, Egerton wondered if there was more to Grundy's death than they knew.

Exhumation

According to Grundy's death certificate, the woman had died of natural causes. However, Egerton knew the only way to rule out foul play was to exhume her body. In England, exhumations of recent deaths were rare. The Greater Manchester Police department had never exhumed a body. "We couldn't find an officer who had ever been involved in such an operation," said Detective Superintendent Bernard Postles.[1] Instead, the police brought in exhumation specialists to help with the body removal.

"A LIFETIME OF HELPING OTHERS"

In the cemetery behind Hyde Chapel, Kathleen Grundy's headstone reads, "Died unexpectedly after a lifetime of helping others."[3] The headstone's inscription is a simple tribute to Grundy, who served the people of Hyde both when she was alive and after her death. It was Grundy's death that set in motion the investigation that stopped serial killer Harold Shipman.

Before they could move forward, the police needed approval from the coroner, John Pollard, to remove Grundy's body from Hyde Cemetery. Egerton went to Pollard's office with the case. He submitted all the evidence he had gathered, including Woodruff's concerns about her mother's death and the questions that had previously been raised against Shipman.

Pollard considered the evidence. "I had to balance all those factors against any distress, not just to the family but to the community. Exhuming bodies always causes distress, and I was aware of that," said Pollard.[2] After reviewing the case, Pollard agreed that police needed to examine Grundy's body. He ordered an exhumation.

Night at the Cemetery

A small team of police officers and exhumation specialists met at Hyde Chapel on August 1, 1998. They began their work at about 2:00 a.m. By working in the middle of the

Grundy died just a week before her eighty-second birthday.

night, they would not disrupt the normal operations of the cemetery and would also cause less distress for the community.

The weather that night was wet, windy, and cold. The men from the exhumation company had a small mechanical digger, but heavy rain slowed their progress. The men worked as quickly as possible in the difficult conditions. As they dug, they placed soil on boards so they did not disturb nearby graves or muddy the cemetery. Crime scene officers carefully collected soil samples from around the coffin. The samples would be used to rule out any potential contamination from the soil.

The three funeral directors who buried Grundy were also at the cemetery. When the exhumation specialists brought up Grundy's coffin, the funeral directors confirmed the correct coffin had been exhumed. They inspected the coffin's brass nameplate, which a crime scene officer removed and placed in a plastic bag.

As the men finished their work, Egerton received a radio call. The operator told him that the staff of Laurel Bank Nursing Home, which overlooked the cemetery, had called police emergency operators to report activity in the graveyard. The police reassured the staff that the nighttime activity was legitimate.

WHAT IS A FORENSIC PATHOLOGIST?

A forensic pathologist is an expert in determining a person's cause of death. These professionals also determine if a death was natural, accidental, or a homicide. This is called the manner of death. Forensic pathologists examine the bodies of people who die suddenly, unexpectedly, or violently. They perform autopsies and look for disease, injury, and poisoning. They collect medical evidence such as body fluids and trace evidence. Forensic pathologists also recreate how a person was injured, interpret those injuries, and estimate the time of death.

Examining the Body

After Grundy's body was exhumed, it was transported to Tameside General Hospital. Forensic pathologist

John Rutherford examined the body. He told Detective Egerton that he could see no apparent physical cause for Grundy's death. Her heart appeared healthy, and there was no evident damage to any of her other organs. Rutherford noted that Grundy appeared in excellent shape for an 81-year-old.

Rutherford was also unable to find any puncture marks that could indicate Grundy had received an injection. However, he noted it was still possible that Grundy had been injected with an unknown substance. "If it's a fine needle, it's likely to leave less in the way of marks than a large needle," he said.[4]

Rutherford collected tissue samples and sent them to the North West Forensic Science Laboratories in Chorley, Lancashire, for testing. Julie Evans, a toxicologist at the forensic laboratory, conducted a series of tests on the samples. She looked to see if any drugs, poisons, or other toxic substances were present. Evans warned the police that her work could take several weeks, as there were many poisons to test for, some of which were hard to detect. "But if Shipman's been really stupid, he would

"I think that [Shipman] probably thought that he could do anything. I think that he thought he was God."[5]

–Angela Woodruff, daughter of Kathleen Grundy

MORPHINE

Morphine is a type of opioid drug. Opioids are made from opium poppy flowers. They are strong drugs that are typically used as painkillers. Opioids work by blocking the pain messages that nerves send to the brain. Morphine can be given in the form of tablets, liquids, or injections. Because morphine is strong and addictive, it can only be prescribed by a doctor.

have used diamorphine," Evans told police.[6] Diamorphine is a drug that breaks down into morphine, which can be easily detected in tissue testing.

Murder Confirmed

On September 2, Evans sent the police her report. Her analysis of Grundy's tissue samples had revealed the woman's cause of death. Evans found elevated levels of morphine in Grundy's liver. The levels were similar to those found in overdose cases. Evans estimated that Grundy died within three hours of receiving the fatal morphine dose.

The police now had confirmation of their suspicions. Kathleen Grundy had been murdered. Even more, the police knew the killer had used morphine to do the job. That piece of knowledge would make investigating future cases easier. Police were ready to find Grundy's killer. But none of them realized they had stumbled upon one of the most prolific serial killers in history.

FORENSIC SPOTLIGHT

Toxicology

Toxicology is the study of how chemicals affect living things. Forensic toxicology detects whether drugs or poisons are present in a person's body. The science is used to determine whether drugs or poisons caused changes in a person's behaviors or contributed to death. In a police investigation, forensic toxicology is used to identify crimes where poisons or drugs are used.

Forensic pathologists collect specimens during an autopsy. Specimens can include samples of blood, urine, hair, liver tissue, stomach contents, and other fluids and tissues. To prevent contamination, all specimens must be correctly labeled and sealed as soon as they are collected. Specially trained scientists called toxicologists use high-tech laboratory equipment to test specimens.

Typically, a series of tests is run to detect the presence of drugs, alcohol, and toxins. One of the most common drug screening tests uses antibodies that detect a reaction with specific substances. This type of testing, called immunoassay screening, will reveal if a specimen is positive or negative for a specific drug. Toxicologists interpret the test results.

Toxicology analysis can take up to 12 weeks.

CHAPTER 2

CHILDHOOD AND EARLY INFLUENCES

On January 14, 1946, Harold Frederick Shipman was born in Nottingham, England. He was the second child of Vera and Harold Shipman. Their daughter, Pauline, was eight years old when the younger Harold was born. In 1950, the Shipman family welcomed a third child, a son named Clive.

The Shipman family lived in a working-class neighborhood. Harold Sr. was a truck driver, delivering stones and other materials for local building companies. Vera stayed at home, keeping the house spotless and raising the Shipman children. Although the family often kept to

Researchers have examined Harold Shipman's childhood, searching for clues about why he became a serial killer.

themselves, those who knew them said they appeared happy and normal.

Harold Sr. and Vera came from working-class families. Harold Sr.'s father worked in a warehouse, Vera's father worked as a bricklayer, and Vera's mother worked in textiles. Harold Sr. appeared content with his life. He worked hard on the job and at home but did not display much ambition. When not working, Harold Sr. enjoyed relaxing in the family garden and smoking his pipe.

An Ambitious Mother

Unlike Harold Sr., Vera had great ambitions for her children. She raised the Shipman children to believe they were better than their peers. It was common for neighborhood children to play outside after school and during holidays. Groups of children gathered and kicked balls, skipped ropes, and played games of jacks and marbles. The Shipman children, however, rarely joined them.

"I knew them well because I lived opposite," said Hannah Cutler, a neighbor of the Shipman family in Nottingham. "I've known the children since they were little. They never mixed with other kids, they didn't play in the street, and when they came home from school, they stayed in the house. I think Harold and Vera wanted them to be different: they didn't want them to be like other kids on the estate, they wanted something better for them. In a way, they were investing in their children."[1]

Of the three children, Harold, known as Fred or Freddie, showed the most promise as a child. He was clever, and his mother was convinced he had a bright future ahead of him. Vera insisted on being very involved in her son's life.

She was often overprotective and controlling, choosing his clothes and friends. At Burford Infants School, eight-year-old Fred wore a bow tie, while the other boys his age wore casual clothes. The bow tie was Vera's idea, as she thought it made the boy look smart. It was an accessory that he would continue to wear throughout his life.

Growing up, Fred was close with his sister and brother but made few other friends. Alan Goddard was one of his

ENGLAND'S SCHOOL SYSTEM

In England, children begin the first stage of education, primary school, at about five years old. The primary school years are divided into infant school and then junior school. Around age 11, students move to secondary school. Some students end their secondary schooling around age 16 and start an apprenticeship. Others move on to sixth form, a two-year program before university.

only childhood friends. Goddard lived near the Shipman family, and he and Fred were in the same class at school. Goddard remembered Fred as a quiet kid who kept to himself most of the time. "There would often be scuffles between different boys on the school bus, but he never joined in," Goddard recalled. "He would never say boo to a goose—he was quiet and kept out of the way of rougher kids. I think the family was quite disciplined, and he stayed at home."[2]

Years at High Pavement

Fred was a bright student in his early school years, and in 1957 he was selected to attend High Pavement, a highly regarded secondary school for boys ages 11 through 18. The Shipmans were very proud that their son was attending High Pavement. However, Fred's academic career at High Pavement was unexceptional. He had gone from being one of the smartest in his class to one of many good students at High Pavement.

Although he did not stand out academically, Fred was a disciplined, model student at High Pavement. He never got in trouble like some of the other boys for swearing, making rude noises, telling dirty jokes, or other foolishness. While other classmates received detention for misbehaving, Fred was never a problem. He was shy and awkward around girls and showed little interest in clothes or music like other boys his age.

Where Fred did excel was in sports. He had a natural talent for rugby and became an important part of the school's team. Fred was tough and aggressive on the field, earning praise for his play. "I was very surprised that he didn't carry on with his rugby after school," said classmate Bob Studholme. "He would definitely have been good enough to play for Leeds University. He might even have made it into a minor county side. I can see him now running hard with the ball in his hands, a curving run down the pitch. He could rattle people's teeth: he was an aggressive player. He was definitely not the same person off the pitch as he was on."[3]

HIGH PAVEMENT SCHOOL

High Pavement was founded in 1788 in Nottingham, England. Over its 200-plus-year history, the school evolved from a charity day school to a boys' secondary school to an advanced school for teens ages 16 to 19. This type of school is called a sixth form college. In 1998, the school became part of Nottingham College.

Fred also did well as a distance runner. By his final year at High Pavement, he was the vice captain of the athletics team. To his teammates, Fred was generally quiet.

Fred, *pictured*, was recognized several times in his school magazine for his athletic skill.

He would join them at the pub after a match or competition but never drank. Classmate Michael Heath saw Fred as a role model because he worked hard in sports and school. "He achieved everything by hard work," said Heath. "He was very serious, a bit of a loner. He'd smile occasionally, but he took life very seriously."[4]

Vera's Illness

Tragedy struck the Shipman family when Fred was 17. His mother was diagnosed with terminal lung cancer.

At the time, there were few effective cancer treatments, and Vera's health quickly deteriorated. The once vibrant woman grew thin and weak. With his father and sister at work and his younger brother at school, Fred came home from school each day to take care of his ailing mother. They spent the afternoons together, drinking tea as Fred told Vera about his day. For Vera, the time spent with her favorite child was the highlight of her day. Vera's illness brought the mother and son closer than ever.

At the time, hospice care for the terminally ill was rare. Instead, Vera spent her final weeks at home. Fred watched as his mother grew weaker and more emaciated each day. As the cancer progressed, Vera became bedridden. The family's doctor visited the house regularly. To manage her pain, the doctor injected Vera with increasingly large doses of morphine. The morphine made Vera more comfortable in the final stages of her cancer and helped to temporarily ease some of her suffering.

Fred watched by his mother's side as the doctor administered the powerful pain reliever. He saw firsthand the quick effect the drug had on his mother. One minute, Vera was in significant pain, and a few moments later, she was more comfortable. After the morphine took hold, she looked more like the vibrant mother he remembered.

The Death of Vera Shipman

On June 21, 1963, Vera died at home. She was only 43 years old. It was a Friday afternoon, and Vera held on until both her sons had arrived home from school to say their final goodbyes. Fred dealt with his mother's death by pushing himself to physical exhaustion, spending the weekend running nonstop in the pouring rain.

The following Monday, Fred returned to school. He kept his feelings about his mother's death well hidden. When one classmate asked him what he had done over the weekend, Fred matter-of-factly replied that his mother had died. The news stunned Fred's classmates. No one had known that Vera was sick, and they were shocked to hear that she had died.

A number were also puzzled by Fred's stoic reaction, as he appeared almost entirely unaffected by her death. Fred did not talk about Vera's death again but wore a black armband on the day of her funeral. Classmate Bob Studholme was stunned by the tragedy, feeling as if Vera's death had come out of nowhere.

"I was closely associated with Fred, playing with him on the rugby team, but he said nothing to me," Studholme recalled. "Other boys would talk about their mothers. . . . He never mentioned his family at all. It wasn't because he was ashamed of his working-class background, because there were so many of us with the same kind of roots."[5]

Vera's death had a profound impact on Fred. It proved to be a turning point in his life. Up until his mother's death, Fred had expressed no interest in studying medicine. Vera's death changed this. The time Fred had spent caring for his mother and watching the doctors and nurses work sparked his interest in the medical field. At age 17, Fred decided he wanted to become a doctor. He wanted to help others, just as the family doctor had helped his mother.

FATHER'S DEATH

Shipman's father, Harold, died suddenly in January 1985 from a heart attack. At work, Shipman appeared unaffected by his father's death and did not take time off for the funeral. Harold Sr. left the family home in Nottingham to Shipman's sister, Pauline, who lived in the house. After her father's death, Pauline sold the home and used the proceeds to buy a house that she shared with her brother Clive and his family. Fred being left out of the inheritance caused a rift between him and his siblings. It further isolated Fred from his extended family.

CHAPTER 3

INTEREST IN MEDICINE

After his mother's death, Shipman focused on his new goal: becoming a doctor. To attend medical school in England, students needed to pass a set of science-heavy exams called A-levels.

In the summer of 1964, Shipman failed to get the grades to go to the school of medicine at the University of Leeds in Leeds, England. Undeterred, he applied himself to his studies and retook the exams in November. This time, Shipman passed the exams and was admitted to the competitive university.

Harold Shipman worked tirelessly to become a doctor.

Studying Medicine

In September 1965, Shipman started his medical studies at the Leeds School of Medicine. Leeds is about a two-hour train ride north of Nottingham. For Shipman, the new city was an exciting place. It was the first time he had lived away from his home and family. Shipman was ready to explore his newfound independence.

Shipman lived with another first-year medical student, Peter Congdon, in a suburb of Leeds. The two men rode the bus to the city center to attend school each day. Medical students spent five years at the university and were required to spend one year working in a hospital as a junior doctor. The program was very intense, and students had little free time for anything other than studying.

A-LEVELS

Advanced Level qualifications (A-levels) are subject-based qualifications in the United Kingdom for students ages 16 and older. Students study A-level subjects over two years. Then they take exams to show their knowledge. Passing A-levels is a requirement to attend many universities in the United Kingdom and other countries. Most universities require students to pass a minimum of three subjects.

Classmates described Shipman as small, thin, and well-dressed. Although he could be blunt sometimes, he did not seek attention. Susan Pearson trained with Shipman at Leeds. "He was quiet," she recalled. "He liked to be part of the group; he wasn't reclusive or isolated. But he wasn't one of the noisy ones. Somehow, he seemed more mature than the rest of us. He didn't seem to be as worried about the amount of work we had to do. It was such a grueling course that a lot of people dropped out, and others seemed to be permanently exhausted. Freddie seemed to cope better than most."[1]

The medical students often experimented on each other as part of their studies. They measured oxygen consumption, did blood tests, and more. In one experiment, Shipman and the other students tested morphine to monitor its effects. Years after Shipman watched the drug soothe his mother's pain, he was finally administering the substance himself.

Romance with Primrose

During his first year of medical school, 19-year-old Shipman met Primrose Oxtoby. Oxtoby was 16. She came from the nearby town of Wetherby. Like Shipman, she was from a strict, working-class family.

After completing a yearlong college course, Oxtoby found work in Leeds creating displays in store windows. To go to work, she rode the bus from Wetherby to Leeds. On one of her bus rides, she met Shipman.

It took weeks of shared bus rides for Shipman, *left*, and Oxtoby, *right*, to gather up the nerve to speak to each other.

Shipman and Oxtoby's romance developed on their shared bus rides. Shy glances and early conversations led to lively banter and a first date. They eventually became a couple. By the end of Shipman's first year at Leeds, Oxtoby was pregnant.

The couple's families were dismayed by the news of Oxtoby's pregnancy. However, they gathered to see Shipman and Primrose get married in a quick legal ceremony on November 5, 1966. The 17-year-old bride was five months pregnant.

On February 14, 1967, when Shipman was a second-year medical student, Primrose gave birth to a baby girl, Sarah Rosemary. This added more stress to an already difficult time in Shipman's life. Money was tight as his student grant was stretched thin by a wife and baby, and Primrose had given up her job as a window dresser.

While his classmates could relax at a pub after class, Shipman went home to his family. Finding time to study between classes and caring for a baby was challenging. However, friends who visited the Shipmans' apartment described the family as happy.

Despite Shipman's busy schedule, he did well in school. He even found time to do clinical work at local hospitals. Classmates described him as diligent, hardworking, and agreeable. In 1970, 24-year-old Shipman graduated from Leeds. He found a position working as a junior doctor at Pontefract General Infirmary.

PRIMROSE OXTOBY

Primrose Oxtoby grew up in a strict Methodist household, the younger of two daughters. She was known as quiet and plain but pleasant to all who knew her. In September 1964, 15-year-old Primrose started a college course at Leeds to study art. Primrose combined her art classes with catering at her mother's urging and learned to decorate cakes professionally. Her first year at college helped Primrose become more independent of her parents. She was determined that her life would be more exciting than theirs.

Working at Pontefract

The life of a junior doctor was difficult. Junior doctors worked long shifts and were expected to handle all types of medical procedures and emergencies. After completing a training year, doctors were fully registered with the United Kingdom's General Medical Council.

Shipman earned his full registration after his first year at Pontefract. He stayed an additional two and a half years, earning special diplomas in child health, obstetrics, and gynecology. While at Pontefract, the Shipmans welcomed a second child, Christopher, in April 1971. Money was still tight, and Shipman rarely socialized with other junior doctors at the pubs. When not at home, he was often studying in the hospital library. He earned extra money during holidays and off-hours working in the hospital's emergency department or filling in for doctors at a nearby hospital.

While working at Pontefract, Shipman became addicted to pethidine, an opioid drug similar to morphine. At the time, pethidine was a popular painkiller given to women during childbirth. It would have been easy for Shipman to prescribe overly large doses for his patients and save the excess for himself. At the time, no one at the hospital noticed anything unusual.

Move to Todmorden

In 1974, Shipman joined a general medical practice in Todmorden in northern England. The practice had three additional full-time doctors and one part-time doctor. It was one of only two general medicine practices in town and served most of the city's 15,000 residents.[2] The doctors were extremely busy, and they were happy to add Shipman as another general practitioner (GP).

In Todmorden, Shipman quickly established a good relationship with his patients and fellow doctors. "He was young, enthusiastic, full of energy, and anxious to do more than he was paid for," said Michael Grieve, one of the practice's senior partners. "He taught the rest of us a lot

Decades later, a report found that Shipman may have killed up to 15 people during his time at Pontefract General Infirmary.

During Shipman's time at Todmorden, he issued more death certificates than any other general practitioner in the region.

because he was the last out of medical school and knew all the latest methods."[3]

The Shipmans enjoyed entertaining friends at their home. Primrose was a good cook and prepared excellent meals for their guests. Neighbors noted that while the house may have been cluttered, it was clean, and the Shipman children were well-behaved. Primrose was quick to smile and pleasant to be around.

Shipman was slightly more aloof and sometimes had a superior air about him. Still, he was always willing to listen to a person's symptoms and give helpful advice.

People who knew him said he was a very dedicated and caring doctor.

However, some of the medical staff in his office had a different view of the young doctor. Some recalled Shipman as rude, noting that he called people he didn't like "stupid."[4] They noted that Shipman could be confrontational and sometimes belittled or embarrassed others. Some said he insisted on getting things done the way he wanted, even though he was one of the least experienced doctors in the practice.

Problems Surface

The first sign that something was amiss occurred in February 1975, almost a year after Shipman began working in Todmorden. Local authorities noticed that Shipman was getting large amounts of pethidine from local pharmacies. They spoke to the pharmacists but were assured that Shipman was a highly regarded local doctor. At the time, the authorities concluded that there was no drug abuse by Shipman but promised to keep an eye on the situation.

In May 1975, Shipman began to have blackouts and seizures. For the first time, the other doctors in his practice began to suspect something was wrong. They insisted

Shipman see a specialist. After a consultation, the specialist incorrectly diagnosed Shipman with epilepsy, a brain disorder that causes seizures. Shipman used the diagnosis to cover up his drug use.

However, the truth came out when the staff realized that Shipman had written many suspicious prescriptions for pethidine for patients and for the practice to keep on hand. While the prescriptions were not unusual, the amounts were larger than needed. One of the practice doctors, John Dacre, investigated the prescriptions and discovered that many patients on the list had never received the drug.

Dacre called a staff meeting and confronted Shipman with his findings. "We were sat round with Fred sitting on one side, and up comes John on the opposite and says, 'Now young Fred, can you explain this?' And he puts before him evidence that he has been gleaning, showing that young Fred had been prescribing pethidine to patients and they'd never received the pethidine, and in fact the pethidine had found its way into Fred's very own veins," recalled Grieve.[5]

Faced with the evidence, Shipman confessed to his drug use and begged his partners for another chance. His only explanation was that he had become interested in drugs and their effects in college. However, when they insisted he leave the practice and seek help, Shipman became angry and left the meeting in a rage. He was forced to resign and get treatment for his pethidine addiction.

Shipman also faced prosecution on several drug offenses and prescription forgery. In February 1976, he was convicted and fined about 650 British pounds, the equivalent of nearly $5,400 in today's currency.[6] The General Medical Council, the governing body of doctors, was told of Shipman's conviction. The council could suspend him or bar him from practicing medicine. After a review of his case, the council decided to suspend Shipman from practicing medicine for a little less than a year. However, they warned Shipman that future offenses would be viewed much more harshly.

GENERAL MEDICAL COUNCIL

The General Medical Council is a public organization that registers and regulates doctors and other medical practitioners in the United Kingdom. The council's primary purpose is to protect public health and safety. It controls which medical professionals are added to the registry and can suspend or remove members as needed. The council also establishes medical school standards in the United Kingdom.

CHAPTER 4

A TRUSTED DOCTOR

Shipman left Todmorden in disgrace. He traveled to York, where he spent six months in a psychiatric facility getting support for his drug addiction. Then, after waiting out his 294-day ban from practicing medicine, he took a job as a clinical medical officer more than 100 miles (160 km) away in County Durham.[1] This role involved working with the South-West Durham Health Authority and local doctors to improve children's health care.

For 18 months, Shipman's work record was spotless. He worked hard, intent on returning to general practice. Then, he

During Shipman's time as a clinical medical officer, he had no access to drugs.

spotted a job advertisement for a medical practice in Hyde.

Move to Hyde

Shipman arrived in Hyde in 1977. One of the partners of the Donneybrook Medical Centre was retiring, leaving an opening for a new doctor. Shipman was one of several applicants who interviewed for the position. During his interview, Shipman freely admitted to the doctors that he'd had a pethidine addiction and had gotten into legal trouble over it. But Shipman assured them that he was no longer taking the drug. Shipman impressed the practice doctors with his candor and qualifications. They hired him on a six-month trial basis.

The Shipmans purchased a modest home about 15 minutes from Hyde's city center. There, the family welcomed two more children. David was born in 1979, and Sam was born in 1982.

Even as Shipman's family was growing, work remained his priority. He often stayed long after the other doctors had left for the evening. His hard work paid off. He quickly built a list of approximately 2,300 patients, one of the largest in the practice. "He was well-liked by patients because he put himself out for them. He'd volunteer

The Shipmans' neighbors described the Shipman children as well-behaved and polite.

to visit them," said Ian Napier, one of the Donneybrook partners. "It made a very heavy workload, but he didn't seem to mind. He was everybody's idea of an old-fashioned doctor."[2]

John Smith, one of the founding members of the Donneybrook practice, felt that Shipman was a kindred spirit. They had similar attitudes and interests. Smith enjoyed Shipman's sense of humor and shared frequent laughs with him. Smith also remembered Shipman being kind and gentle with his patients.

Shipman's Other Side

Although Shipman was pleasant with his patients, he could be rude and demanding with the nonmedical staff

"No one else was up to his standard. You could not tell him anything and he was never wrong."[4]

—A former staff member at the Donneybrook medical practice

at his office. He constantly found fault with some of the staff and resented anyone who stood up to his directions. When he disliked someone, he ordered the practice manager, Vivien Langfield, to fire them. He reduced drug sales representatives to tears. And while he was generally polite to the other doctors, Shipman mocked them behind their backs.

Shipman's mean-spirited attacks were often delivered as sarcasm. He never yelled but spoke in a quiet and controlled voice. "He was a bully who demanded that people look up to him and have regard to his position," said Langfield. "If anyone queried anything to do with one of his patients, he would say, 'I am a good doctor. I have all the qualifications from Leeds Medical School. I have passed my exams,' implying that you had better listen to him."[3]

Over the years, Shipman became more forceful with his colleagues. He got annoyed if the other doctors did not agree with his proposals. Although he and his fellow doctors were partners in the practice, Shipman believed that his views were superior. "He could be arrogant," admitted Napier, "but I was never aware of him falling down diagnostically. I think he was a sound doctor. His main failing was that he always had to prove he knew more and was better than anyone else."[5]

Another partner, Geoffrey Bills, noticed that Shipman often exaggerated his patients' conditions. If a patient had a chest infection, Shipman described it as pneumonia. He believed Shipman exaggerated to make himself look good when the patient got better. Bills noticed that Shipman often bragged to the other doctors about his success in treating patients with heart disease. He also noted that Shipman was quick to prescribe medications for patients.

A FAMILY DIVIDED

Edna and George Oxtoby were never fond of their son-in-law, but they tolerated Shipman for their daughter's sake. When the Shipmans left Todmorden, the Oxtobys provided a home for Primrose and her children for several months. However, the relationship between Primrose and her parents became irreparably damaged. The Oxtobys were clear with Primrose that they believed marrying Shipman was a mistake. Once Shipman was back on his feet, Primrose and the children left the Oxtoby home. She cut off all communication with her parents.

An Old-Fashioned Doctor

By the mid-1980s, most of the doctors in the Donneybrook practice had stopped making regular house calls. Shipman, however, never stopped his regular home visits with his elderly patients. Many of his patients loved this hands-on approach.

In contrast, Shipman was much less sociable with his partners. He would attend the occasional farewell party but rarely joined his coworkers for golf, drinks, or meals. Unlike in their younger years, the Shipmans did not host dinners for their Hyde neighbors.

In the 1990s, the British government required all medical practices to computerize their records. Although Shipman never liked being told what to do, he realized that computers were becoming increasingly important. He began to push for computers at the Donneybrook practice. Although he had only superficial computer skills, Shipman acted like an expert.

During Shipman's years at Donneybrook, there were some unexpected patient deaths. However, Shipman's partners noticed nothing out of the ordinary. The patients were elderly, and although their deaths were earlier than expected, they did not raise suspicion at the time.

Starting a Solo Practice

In 1992, Shipman announced that he was leaving the Donneybrook Medical Centre to start his own medical practice. His partners were surprised, but Shipman had been planning his exit carefully. Although he had signed a partnership agreement, he found a loophole that allowed him to leave and take his patient list with him.

In July 1992, Shipman opened his new office on Market Street in Hyde. It was located on a block with several shops and restaurants. He hired three receptionists, a computer operator, and a nurse. Primrose supported her husband, working at the reception desk on Saturdays and whenever a receptionist was sick.

On his own, Shipman could practice medicine however he wanted with no one looking over

Shipman's new medical practice was just a two-minute walk from the Donneybrook Medical Centre.

his shoulder. He decorated his office to his taste, filling the space with pictures of pigs, steam engines, and a large caricature of his face.

Shipman also became more arrogant. At Donneybrook, he had generally been polite to his colleagues. At his own practice, he became more bad-tempered and rude, even to his fellow doctors. Owning his own business had inflated Shipman's ego, and he believed himself to be more superior than ever.

"There's nobody to challenge you," said Wally Ashworth, a doctor who worked with Shipman on a local medical committee, about owning a practice. "You can convince yourself that you know it all. Your patients look up to you as if you are God. Lots of GPs are puffed up with their own image: it's a job that takes you up a peg or two, not down a peg or two."[6]

Despite Shipman's prickly demeanor, Ashworth and the rest of the medical community had no reason to suspect anything was wrong in Shipman's practice. They believed he was a good doctor who treated his patients well. Shipman's patients and their families agreed and trusted the doctor with their care. They appreciated his old-fashioned, hands-on approach. He spent time with them, made house calls, and treated everyone warmly.

"He'd go far beyond the normal call of duty for a GP," said nurse Kate McGraw. "One of the patients lost a thumb and finger in an accident. When he arrived home from the hospital he was in great pain, and Fred spent hours at his home, constructing a makeshift sling, and just talking to him for half the night. He'd call in on patients on the way home from work and on his way into work in the morning. If he was worried about someone, he'd call."[7] As a result, there was a long waiting list of people who wanted to see Shipman.

RENATE OVERTON

In April 1995, Renate Overton had an asthma attack at home. She called her family doctor, Shipman. Shipman injected Overton with morphine, likely in an attempt to kill her, but Overton did not die immediately. Instead, she fell into a coma. She died 14 months later. Instead of questioning why Shipman had given his patient morphine, the pathologist who performed Overton's autopsy ruled that the woman died of natural causes.

CHAPTER 5

FIRST SUSPICIONS

Not everyone in Hyde trusted Shipman. John Shaw drove a taxi in Hyde. Many of his regular passengers were older women whom he drove to the post office, the grocery store, bingo games, and coffee clubs. The women relied on Shaw to carry their shopping bags and perform basic repairs to their homes, such as changing light bulbs. Shaw enjoyed the work and became fond of his regulars. He got to know them all personally.

In the past, an elderly customer would die from time to time. It was always sad, and Shaw would often pay his respects at

Shipman killed many of his victims at his practice.

John Shaw worked as a taxi driver in Hyde from 1988 to 1998.

the funeral. But over the years, deaths became more frequent. Even stranger was that many of Shaw's regulars were dying in nearly identical ways. One day, they were active and healthy, and the next day they had died. Often, the women had just visited their doctor. In other cases, the doctor had made a house call and discovered them dead, sitting on a chair or sofa.

Shaw grew increasingly concerned. By 1996, a customer was dying every three or four weeks. He started keeping a list of customers who had died. He also began asking their families who their doctor was. It was always Shipman. Shaw felt uneasy and talked with his wife, Kath, about what he should do. "I'd say, 'I've got to tell someone,'" recalled Shaw. "And Kath would say: 'If you do go to the police, you'll be ridiculed. If you're wrong, you'll get taken to court for libel-slander.'"[1] Shaw decided to stay quiet. He was convinced no one would believe him.

A Pattern Emerges

Meanwhile, Debbie Bambroffe began to have suspicions about Shipman. Bambroffe worked as an undertaker at her family's business, Frank Massey & Son. She worked alongside her husband, David Bambroffe, and father, Alan Massey. The Massey family business was founded in 1903 by Alan's grandfather. It was a well-known family business in the Hyde community.

By late 1997, Bambroffe had noticed an unusual pattern. The funeral home had seen an increase in the deaths of older women, all of whom were patients of Shipman. Shipman had a lot of elderly patients, so it was not entirely unexpected that he would have more patient deaths than doctors with younger patients.

However, other details concerned Bambroffe. Many of the dead patients were found sitting up in chairs, fully dressed. Years of experience as a funeral director had taught Bambroffe that death was often unexpected. People who died of unexpected heart attacks were often found on the floor. If they had been sick for some time, they were usually found in bed wearing bedclothes. "Of course, there are people who die peacefully in their armchairs, so finding one or two bodies like that would not cause any surprise," said Bambroffe. "It was the fact that they were all in that position."[2]

Bambroffe and her family discussed their suspicions. It was hard to think someone as trusted and respected as Shipman could kill his patients. But Bambroffe was sure that something was wrong. She decided to speak about her concerns with Susan Booth. Booth was a doctor at the Brooke Surgery, across the street from Shipman's office. The next time Booth came to countersign a cremation form for Shipman, Bambroffe pulled her aside and explained her concerns. Booth promised to talk to her partners about the matter.

CREMATION FORMS

After death, a body can be released for cremation only after the patient's doctor fills out a form detailing the patient's cause of death. A second doctor must confirm the cause of death and countersign the form. As part of this process, the second doctor often visits wherever the body is being held. The doctors at the Brooke Surgery in Hyde often countersigned cremation forms for Shipman's patients.

More Suspicions

The Brooke partners met at a pub outside Hyde so no one

Several of the family members who owned Frank Massey & Son were also Shipman's patients.

from town would overhear their conversation. One of the partners, Linda Reynolds, had suspicions about Shipman. "I think he has to be harming them. I think he could be causing the deaths," she said.[3] Yet the doctors were concerned about confronting Shipman.

"We knew he was quite well connected with the local health authority," said Raj Patel, another Brooke partner. "He knew people there on first name terms, people in positions of power."[4] The Brooke doctors did not want Shipman to retaliate against them.

The Brooke doctors considered reporting Shipman to the health authority, but they worried he would

John Pollard began working as a coroner in Manchester, England, in 1982.

find out. Instead, Reynolds called a doctors' insurance group, but they could do nothing without proof. She next called the General Medical Council, which was supposed to police doctors. However, she was told the council could not act without an official complaint.

Frustrated with the lack of progress, Reynolds called John Pollard, the South Manchester coroner. Pollard agreed to contact the Greater Manchester Police to look into Shipman's practice. Reynolds requested that the police not tell Shipman about their inquiry. Pollard agreed.

A Flawed Investigation

The Greater Manchester Police opened a discreet investigation into Shipman in March 1998. Detective Inspector Dave Smith was assigned to the case. One of his first actions was to interview Reynolds, who told him about her concerns. She also told Smith that the bodies of two Shipman patients were waiting for cremation. However, Smith never requested an autopsy on these bodies. Had he done so, the coroner may have found the presence of morphine and linked it to their deaths.

"There were two alternatives. On the one hand, Dr. Shipman could have been a most evil person who was killing his patients; on the other, he could have been a very good doctor who just happened to be there with his elderly patients when they died."[6]

—John Pollard, coroner, on the March 1998 investigation

Next, Smith requested six months of death certificates for Shipman's patients. During that period, 28 patients had died. But the Tameside Register Office sent records for only 19 deaths. Smith then requested the West Pennine Health Authority compare the causes of death with the medical records of the 19 patients.[5]

Smith met with Alan Banks, a medical adviser to the Health Authority, to discuss the medical records.

Banks failed to find anything unusual with Shipman's medical records. However, his prior knowledge and respect for Shipman may have biased his review.

"Dr. Banks erroneously concluded that there was no 'pattern' to be found," Janet Smith, a judge involved in Shipman's case, later wrote. "He failed to see the unusual features which characterized many of the deaths. If he did notice anything which struck him as odd, he immediately found an innocent explanation for it. He approached his examination of the records in the belief that there would be no cause for concern and was simply unable to open his mind to the possibility that Shipman might have harmed a patient."[7]

THE MOORS MURDERERS

Harold Shipman was not Manchester's first serial killer. Between July 1963 and October 1965, Ian Brady and Myra Hindley murdered five children and teenagers. They buried their victims on Saddleworth Moor and became known as the Moors Murderers. The pair was arrested in October 1965. Both were found guilty of murder and sentenced to life in prison.

Dave Smith's investigation lasted only four weeks. After speaking with his supervisor, Chief Superintendent David Sykes, Smith concluded that there was no substance to the concerns raised by Reynolds about Shipman. He closed the investigation in April 1998. He did not make a written report of the investigation. He also never checked to see whether Shipman had any previous convictions. If he had, he would have uncovered Shipman's drug and forgery offenses from his time in Todmorden.

Although the investigation into Shipman was carried out discreetly, there were indications that Shipman found out about it. Afterward, he never again asked the Brooke doctors to countersign his cremation forms, although he had relied on them for years prior. Shipman may have paused his murders for a brief time. However, before long, deaths of patients in his care once again suspiciously soared.

POLICE MISTAKES

Years after the March 1998 investigation, a public inquiry found that Shipman's final three murders could have been prevented if the investigation had been handled correctly. The inquiry found that Detective Inspector Dave Smith did not fully understand the case and failed to ask basic questions, such as whether Shipman had a police record.

CHAPTER 6

DEATH AND FORGERY

Kathleen Grundy was a well-known figure in Hyde. At 81 years old, she was still strong and healthy. Grundy kept a busy social calendar filled with volunteer work for several charities. She was also a longtime Shipman patient, following him from the Donneybrook practice to his solo office on Market Street.

On June 23, 1998, Grundy stopped by Shipman's office to have built-up wax removed from her ears. At the visit, Shipman arranged to stop by Grundy's home the next day for a routine blood test. Later that night, Grundy visited her friend May Clarke.

By the time he murdered Kathleen Grundy, Shipman was killing about one person every week.

She spoke with pride about her grandsons. Grundy also mentioned that Shipman was stopping by the next day.

Grundy was scheduled to serve lunches at a local charity club on June 24. When she did not arrive, her friends became concerned. They decided to stop by her house to check on her. When they arrived, the women found Grundy's door unlocked. They entered the house and discovered her dead on the sofa, fully clothed. They called Shipman.

Shipman arrived at Grundy's home and quickly examined the body. Shipman was the last person to see her alive. He called the local coroner and filled out a death certificate. The certificate listed "old age" as Grundy's cause of death.[1]

The Will of Kathleen Grundy

On the same day, the Hamilton Ward law firm received a typewritten will in the mail. It was from Kathleen Grundy. The will was unexpected, as Grundy was not a client of the law firm. A few days later, a typewritten letter arrived at the firm. The letter had no return address and was signed by a man named Smith. The letter informed the law firm that Grundy had died four days earlier, the same day the typewritten will had arrived at the Hamilton Ward office.

Uncertain whether the will was valid, the Hamilton Ward lawyers contacted Grundy's daughter, Angela Woodruff. They told her about Grundy's new will. Grundy had left her entire estate, worth approximately 386,000 British pounds, the equivalent of $920,000 in today's currency, to Shipman.[2] Woodruff immediately sensed something was wrong. She was a lawyer, so her own law firm in Warwick had always handled her mother's legal needs. The firm had prepared Grundy's original will in 1986. Nothing about the new will made sense to Woodruff.

Woodruff got a copy of the new will. Immediately, she suspected it was a forgery. "My mother was a meticulously tidy person. The thought of her signing

After reading the letter Hamilton Ward had received, Woodruff searched for Smith, the person who signed the letter. No one she spoke to knew the mysterious letter writer.

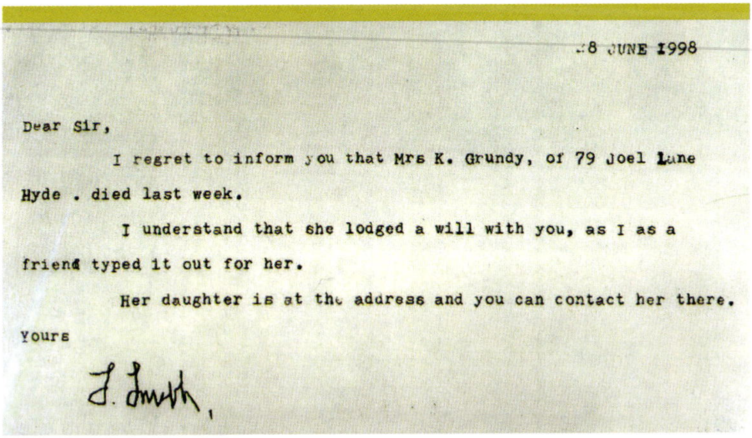

28 JUNE 1998

Dear Sir,

I regret to inform you that Mrs K. Grundy, of 79 Joel Lane Hyde . died last week.

I understand that she lodged a will with you, as I as a friend typed it out for her.

Her daughter is at the address and you can contact her there.

Yours

J. Smith

"I had my suspicions about my mother's will and began to have suspicions about my mother's death—although it was a hard one to believe."[4]

—Angela Woodruff, daughter of Shipman victim Kathleen Grundy

a document which is so badly typed didn't make any sense," said Woodruff. Woodruff also questioned Grundy's signature on the will. "The signature looked strange. It looked too big. The concept of Mum signing a document leaving everything to her doctor was unbelievable," she said.[3]

The will was signed by two witnesses, Claire Hutchinson and Paul Spencer. Both were patients of Shipman. Woodruff spoke to both parties and discovered that about two weeks before Grundy's death, Hutchinson and Spencer were in Shipman's waiting room when Shipman asked if they could witness Grundy's signature on an unknown document. However, when Woodruff showed Hutchinson and Spencer the will, they said the witness signatures did not belong to them.

Alerting the Police

Woodruff took her suspicions to the police. At the time, she had no idea that others also had concerns about the sudden deaths of Shipman's patients. However, Bernard Postles, the detective chief superintendent in Manchester,

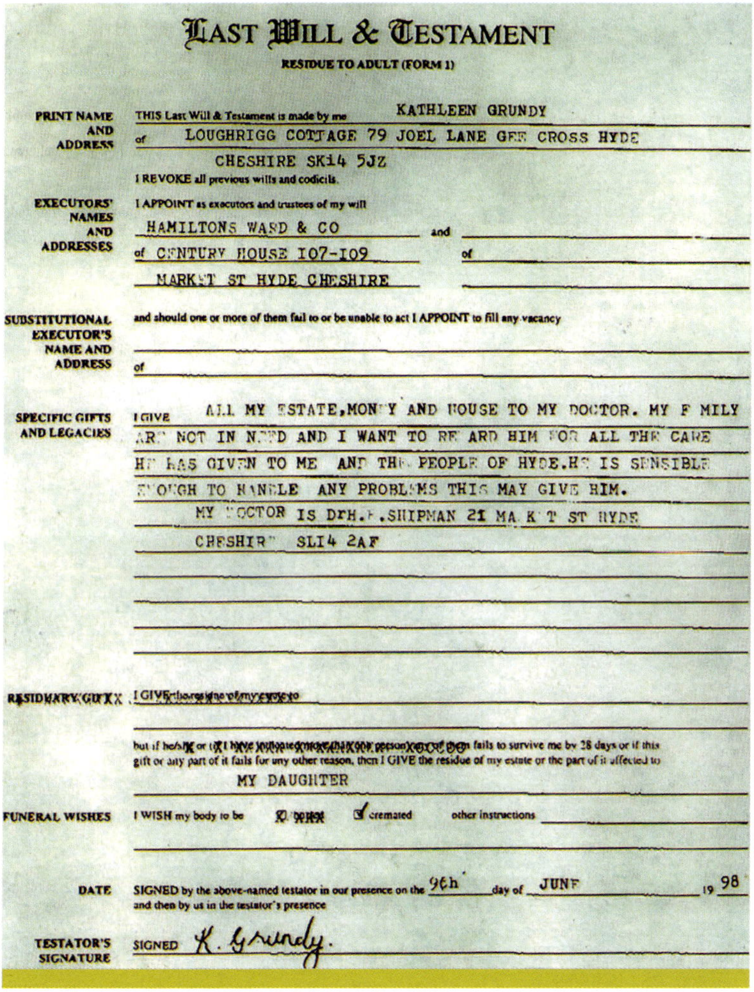

LAST WILL & TESTAMENT

RESIDUE TO ADULT (FORM 1)

PRINT NAME AND ADDRESS — THIS Last Will & Testament is made by me KATHLEEN GRUNDY
of LOUGHRIGG COTTAGE 79 JOEL LANE GEE CROSS HYDE
CHESHIRE SK14 5JZ

I REVOKE all previous wills and codicils.

EXECUTORS' NAMES AND ADDRESSES — I APPOINT as executors and trustees of my will
HAMILTONS WARD & CO and
of CENTURY HOUSE 107-109 of
MARKET ST HYDE CHESHIRE

SUBSTITUTIONAL EXECUTOR'S NAME AND ADDRESS — and should one or more of them fail to or be unable to act I APPOINT to fill any vacancy
of

SPECIFIC GIFTS AND LEGACIES — I GIVE ALL MY ESTATE,MONEY AND HOUSE TO MY DOCTOR. MY FAMILY ARE NOT IN NEED AND I WANT TO REWARD HIM FOR ALL THE CARE HE HAS GIVEN TO ME AND THE PEOPLE OF HYDE.HE IS SENSIBLE ENOUGH TO HANDLE ANY PROBLEMS THIS MAY GIVE HIM.
MY DOCTOR IS DrH.F.SHIPMAN 21 MARKET ST HYDE
CHESHIRE SK14 2AF

RESIDUARY GIFT — I GIVE the residue of my estate to

but if he/she or (if I have indicated more than one person) any of them fails to survive me by 28 days or if this gift or any part of it fails for any other reason, then I GIVE the residue of my estate or the part of it affected to
MY DAUGHTER

FUNERAL WISHES — I WISH my body to be [buried] ✓ cremated other instructions

DATE — SIGNED by the above-named testator in our presence on the 9th day of JUNE 1998
and then by us in the testator's presence

TESTATOR'S SIGNATURE — SIGNED K. Grundy.

Shipman broke down crying to several of his patients, swearing he hadn't forged Grundy's will.

knew about the earlier investigation into Shipman. He suspected that the case involved more than a forged will. He believed Grundy had been murdered. "It sounded like a classic Agatha Christie," he said, referencing the famous mystery novelist. "It fit together too well."[5]

On August 1, 1998, police exhumed Grundy's body. That same day, police searched Shipman's office and home. The search was timed to happen before Shipman heard about Grundy's exhumation. Officers approached Shipman as he was locking up the office after seeing his Saturday patients. Shipman did not seem surprised at the arrival of the officers. He offered to help them in any way and spoke in an arrogant and condescending manner.

The search warrant listed a typewriter as one of the items police sought. When asked about the office equipment, Shipman went to a cabinet and presented the police with a portable typewriter. "Mrs. Grundy borrows it from time to time," Shipman said.[6] Forensic tests later confirmed that Grundy's will and the subsequent letter had been typed on Shipman's typewriter. Forensic testing also found Shipman's fingerprint on the bottom of the will. However, Grundy and the two witnesses had left no fingerprints on the document.

BERNARD POSTLES

Detective Chief Superintendent Bernard Postles led the Shipman investigation. Postles was a former bank employee who became a police officer in 1972. By 1977, Postles had moved into the Criminal Investigation Department, where he worked on the serious crimes squad, drug squad, and major incident unit. In 2001, Postles received the Queen's Police Medal for his work for the Greater Manchester Police.

Another team of officers searched Shipman's home simultaneously to prevent any evidence from being destroyed. The house was filled with filth and mess. Piles of newspapers, dirty clothes, and trash were scattered throughout the home. Although police found nothing related to Grundy's will, they found a significant collection of jewelry, including rings that were too small for Primrose Shipman's fingers.

STOLEN JEWELRY

In the search of Shipman's home, police found more than 30 pieces of jewelry that they suspected the doctor had stolen from his patients.[7] The pieces included rings, earrings, necklaces, and bracelets. Detectives believe that Shipman helped himself to his patients' jewelry and cash after he injected them with morphine. As the jewelry owners were never identified, the police sold the pieces at auction and donated the proceeds to victim support efforts.

Rumors Swirl

Fearing that Shipman could be a killer, the police attempted to stop him from seeing patients. Police called the General Medical Council and requested that they suspend Shipman. However, the council declined because Shipman had not been convicted of a crime. The police also contacted the National Health Service but were told nothing could be done without a lengthy hearing to consider the evidence against Shipman.

In Hyde, word quickly spread about the exhumation of Grundy and the search of Shipman's office. Many people were curious, and gossip began to swirl. However, Shipman appeared confident and unconcerned about the police activity. Meanwhile, most of his patients remained loyal, keeping his office waiting room filled.

PRIMROSE'S SILENCE

It is unknown whether Primrose knew about her husband's murders. Throughout the investigation, Primrose refused to talk. Because she was not under arrest, the police could not force Primrose to answer their questions. She also refused to speak to reporters and slammed the door on television crews. Whenever she was asked a question, she simply responded, "No comment."[9]

By mid-August, word of the investigation spread to the press. When reporters gathered outside Shipman's office, he met them with a smile but deflected all questions to his lawyer. Soon, national newspapers, radio programs, and television news shows carried the story and reported that the deaths of 20 Shipman patients were being investigated.[8] With pressure building, Shipman called Anne Ball, a lawyer at Hempsons law firm, to represent him. Ball had worked on other legal defense cases, but when she took Shipman as a client, she likely had little idea of the magnitude of Shipman's case.

The Investigation Grows

As more people learned of the investigation into Shipman, some began to recognize suspicious circumstances in the deaths of their loved ones. They started making phone calls to the police.

"People began to ring in," said Postles. "Some of these people had harbored concerns about the death of their relative for quite some time, in some cases years, and what they did was, they started to hear the story that was developing in relation to Kathleen Grundy, and started to put two and two together: 'That's very similar to the way that my mother's body was discovered,' for instance . . . and they began to ring in."[10]

"I think the only valid possible explanation for it is that [Harold Shipman] simply enjoyed viewing the process of dying and enjoyed the feeling of control over life and death."[12]

—John Pollard, coroner, on Shipman's motive

On August 21, Postles set up an incident room at the police station. There was no doubt they were about to embark on a significant inquiry. A preliminary look at the deaths of Shipman's patients in the past 12 months had yielded more than 30 names as potential victims.[11] And the police still did not know how far back the killings went.

CHAPTER 7

EXHUMATIONS AND ARREST

As the police opened a broader investigation into Shipman's activities, Postles instructed his team to get copies of all death certificates of Shipman patients who had died in the past year. Working in teams of two, detectives divided up the list of patients. Each team compared death certificates to patients' medical records. They also interviewed friends and family of the deceased.

Deciding which deaths to investigate was important. To choose, the police prioritized deaths that fit specific details and patterns. The highest-priority deaths were those where the patient had died shortly after a house call from Shipman and the body was buried instead of cremated. In these cases, tissue samples could be collected for forensic examination.

For deaths after which the patient had been cremated, police looked for patterns. They compared patients' known preexisting conditions with their recorded causes

During the investigation, detectives were repeatedly reminded that Shipman was innocent until proven guilty—even as evidence mounted against him.

of death. They also looked for cases in which Shipman had made a recent house call.

When the forensic lab confirmed a large amount of morphine in Kathleen Grundy's body on September 2, the police had the evidence they needed to arrest Shipman. They also learned from the forensic toxicologist that morphine does not degrade. That meant that as long as there was tissue to test, morphine could be found, no matter how long ago a person had died. If Shipman had

Irene Turner's body was exhumed on November 10, 1998.

used morphine to kill other patients, it could be detected in those who were buried.

Police Make an Arrest

On September 7, the police arrested Shipman. They charged him with the murder of Kathleen Grundy, attempted theft by deception, and three counts of forgery.[1] During questioning, Shipman remained calm and collected. At times, he was arrogant and condescending. He appeared annoyed at the junior officers questioning him.

Shipman also appeared eager for detectives to examine Grundy's medical records. He was confident the records would support his claim that he'd had nothing to do with Grundy's death. He told the police that he did not keep controlled drugs in his office and therefore did not need a controlled drug register, which is a record of the details of any controlled drugs received or supplied by a pharmacy.

More Exhumations

Between September and December 1998, the police exhumed 12 bodies as part of their investigation.[2] The first, Grundy's body, was reburied about two weeks after being exhumed. However, Postles decided that any additional bodies exhumed would be examined by forensic pathologists and reburied within 24 hours to reduce trauma for the victims' families. The police also got

BAIL DENIED

When someone is arrested, they can often pay an amount of money to be let out of jail until their trial is over. The money is returned after the trial. This is called bail. After Shipman's arrest, Primrose gathered friends to ask for help raising bail money. Many people volunteered to donate, as there was initially strong support for Shipman in the community. Ten days after the arrest, Shipman's lawyers presented the court with a list of people willing to put up significant amounts of money for bail. However, the judge denied bail and decided Shipman would remain in custody until his trial.

permission from each victim's family before exhuming a body. Most families agreed, but if they did not, the police did not proceed.

"We didn't embark on these exhumations speculatively," said Postles. "We investigated the deaths first. We needed proper justification and cause, both for the coroner and the families, to convince them of the need to exhume. It was particularly distressing for the families. It wasn't something anyone was comfortable with."[3]

The police hired a professional exhumation company to recover the bodies. Exhumations began at about 4:00 a.m. to avoid media attention and minimize disruptions to the cemetery's operations. Coroner John Pollard ordered the exhumations. "After the twelfth, I got together with Mr. Postles and we were both of the same mind: that we could carry on ad infinitum and that we should now stop," said Pollard. "We had exhumed sufficient bodies to show the pattern and the modus operandi."[4]

PUBLIC DISBELIEF

For many of Shipman's patients, news of the police investigation into the doctor was met with shock and disbelief. Some detectives faced openly hostile residents who believed Shipman was an excellent doctor. They thought the police were unfairly targeting Shipman. Some felt the police gathered in Hyde were intrusive and that the dead should be left in peace.

Following the Cyber Trail

After Shipman's arrest, detectives from the computer investigative division returned to Shipman's office to gather information from the practice's computer system. When examining Shipman's computer files, the police expert discovered the doctor had been falsifying patient records. He had been making extra entries and changing the dates to make it seem like the notes had been made months before.

The entries added symptoms and ailments to patient records, making it seem like his victims had been more ill than they really were. However, Shipman hadn't realized that the software automatically recorded the actual date

Detective John Ashley found evidence on Shipman's hard drive that the doctor had tampered with patient files.

FORENSIC SPOTLIGHT

Digital Evidence

Digital evidence is any data stored on, received by, or sent by an electronic device. There are many sources of digital evidence, but the most common include computers and mobile devices. Digital forensic experts can gather documents, emails, texts, instant messages, transactions, images, web browsing history, and more from electronic devices. Gathering data from computers and other electronic devices must be done very carefully to prevent losing or destroying information.

To retrieve and analyze digital evidence, forensic analysts first create a copy of the data. This ensures they have a backup if something happens to the original. Analysts may also set up the storage device so that data can be viewed but not changed, added, or deleted, preserving the evidence.

Analysts search for hidden areas on the device and deleted files. Digital evidence can also exist on the internet in chat rooms, websites, and other networks. Analysts use internet addresses, email header information, time stamps, and other data to create a picture of computer and internet activity that can be used as evidence.

People who want to become digital forensic analysts can get degrees in digital forensics, cybersecurity, or computer science.

he'd made each entry. Many of the entries were made soon after patient deaths. This gave investigators a trail to follow.

The evidence was hard to deny. For example, on May 11, 1998, Shipman visited 73-year-old Winifred Mellor. Mellor was found dead later that day, sitting in her chair with her sleeve rolled up, as if to receive an injection.

After Shipman's visit, he returned to his office and made three entries to Mellor's medical records. First, he opened a record for an August 1, 1997, visit for earwax removal and added a note that Mellor complained of chest pain. Next, Shipman added a record of an office visit on January 26, 1998, for chest pain and noted that Mellor refused further testing. In a third entry dated about ten days before Mellor's death, Shipman noted that she had visited his office and reported chest pain but still refused additional testing.

After Mellor's death, Shipman told her grieving daughters that Mellor had chest pain but refused treatment. He assured them that there was no need for an autopsy. He filled out Mellor's death certificate, marking coronary thrombosis, a heart attack, as the cause of death.

Mellor's body was exhumed in September 1998 with the permission of her family. The subsequent autopsy found no evidence of a heart attack as her cause of death. It did, however, find a fatal amount of morphine in her body.

Interrogation and Breakdown

On October 5, the police interrogated Shipman about Mellor's death. At first, Shipman insisted that Mellor had a history of chest pain and stated that she died of a heart attack. When police told him Mellor's autopsy had found no evidence of heart attack, Shipman responded that they could not rule out "an electrical disorganization of the heart which kills you just as effectively and leaves no symptoms at all."[5] When told that Mellor's body had a fatal amount of morphine, Shipman denied injecting her and insisted he had no idea how she got the drug.

"In a million years, you don't expect your doctor to be Britain's worst serial killer. This was someone you trusted with your emotional and physical problems. I think for me personally, the sense of betrayal is sometimes worse than the actual murder."[6]

—Jane Ashton-Hibbert, granddaughter of Shipman victim Hilda Hibbert

However, when the police revealed they had uncovered computer evidence that proved Shipman had altered his patients' medical records, the doctor grew uneasy. It was clear that Shipman never expected the police to find that evidence. Shortly after the questioning about the computer evidence began, Shipman's attorney, Anne Ball, asked for a break to meet with her client. During the break, Shipman broke down and collapsed on the floor, sobbing.

Ball told detectives that Shipman was not fit to continue with questioning. The police called a doctor, who agreed that the interview should be stopped as Shipman's emotional state was unfit. Some officers believed that Shipman's breakdown was simply an act designed to give him more time to think about how he would respond to the police questions and computer evidence. Others thought Shipman became emotional when he realized the amount of evidence stacking up against him.

COVERING UP THE CRIME

Shipman advised many families to cremate their dead loved ones. In each case, he had presented a reasonable cause of death and stressed that no additional investigation would be needed. Even though families were often surprised to learn about the health conditions of their loved ones, most still trusted Shipman's word as a respected doctor. When a family member had questions for Shipman, the doctor provided computerized medical notes that seemed to back up the listed cause of death.

Shipman was formally charged with murder at Tameside Magistrates' Court.

More Charges Filed

On October 7, Shipman appeared in court and was charged with murdering three more people: Joan Melia, Winifred Mellor, and Bianka Pomfret.[7] He pleaded not guilty. Shipman appeared pale and weary. He shook his head, sobbed, and swayed from side to side during the hearing. Two security guards helped him from the court.

In prison, Shipman was put on suicide watch, and officers checked on him hourly. Three days later, however, Shipman had regained his composure. In court again for additional charges related to Grundy, he appeared calm. He even winked at his wife, Primrose, who was sitting in the public gallery.

From then on, the police did not conduct further interviews with Shipman. They felt it would be a waste of time, as he would claim to be emotionally unstable to avoid their questions. A psychologist examined Shipman and determined he understood the charges against him and was fit for trial.

As the police continued to investigate patient deaths, new charges were filed against Shipman. Throughout it all, Shipman never offered an explanation for his actions. Each time new charges were brought against him, he was given the opportunity to respond. He simply responded, "I treated them appropriately for their medical condition at the time."[8] By the time his trial date arrived, Shipman was charged with killing 15 women between 1995 and 1998.[9]

MORPHINE SUPPLIES

Shipman had several methods of obtaining the morphine used in his murders. Sometimes he prescribed morphine to patients who didn't need the drug and used the supplies to carry out murders. He would also overprescribe morphine for patients who needed the drug and use the excess to carry out his crimes. Other times, when terminally ill patients died, Shipman would take possession of any remaining morphine they had.

CHAPTER 8

THE TRIAL BEGINS

The trial of Harold Shipman began on October 5, 1999. The defense had argued Shipman could not get a fair trial in Manchester, so the venue was moved to Preston, a town about 35 miles (56 km) from Hyde. Prosecutors charged Shipman with 15 counts of murder and one count of forgery.[1]

Shipman sat in the court dressed in a light brown suit, white shirt, and dark tie. His wife, Primrose, and two of his children sat in the public gallery. After narrowing a pool of 60 jurors down to 12, the jury was sworn in, and the trial began.[2]

The Prosecution Presents Its Case

Richard Henriques, a senior lawyer, led the prosecution. On October 11, Henriques delivered his opening address and laid out the prosecution's case against Shipman. He claimed that Shipman had murdered his 15 victims

Shipman was driven to his trial under police escort.

by injecting them with large doses of morphine or diamorphine.

"All of them died most unexpectedly," said Henriques. "All of them had seen Dr. Shipman on the day of their death. There is no question of euthanasia or what is sometimes called mercy killing. The defendant killed those 15 patients because, in the submission of the prosecution, he enjoyed doing so. He was exercising the ultimate power of controlling life and death and repeated the act so often he must have found the drama of taking life to his taste."[3]

Henriques detailed the similarities in each of the cases. He explained that Shipman had falsified patient records, advised family members that autopsies were not needed, and done little to examine the deceased. "In several cases, his manner was unsympathetic and inappropriate after death," said Henriques. "When each of these allegations is looked at and placed in the context of the trial as a whole, it will be very plain that Dr. Shipman killed each of these 15 women as he purported to treat them as patients."[4]

The prosecution called the friends and family of the victims as witnesses. The witnesses talked about the victims and told the court how healthy they had been. Their testimonies drew a vivid portrait of the 15 victims and showed they were living fulfilling lives at

SHIPMAN'S LETTERS

Before and during his trial, Shipman wrote a series of letters to a few close friends. Writing helped pass the time in prison. In the letters, Shipman described his days behind bars. He talked about fellow inmates and complained about the prison staff. Once the trial began, Shipman wrote about what happened that day in the courtroom. Throughout it all, he never showed remorse or admitted guilt.

the time of their deaths. Witnesses talked about the last days and hours of the victims' lives.

The prosecution also called several experts to testify. Computer experts explained how Shipman had falsified medical records. Medical experts described the amount of morphine needed to kill and the effects of the drug on the body. An expert from Germany described how morphine could be found in hair samples. Toxicologist Julie Evans testified about the morphine she found in the tissues of the exhumed victims. Pharmacists from Hyde gave evidence about filling prescriptions of morphine and diamorphine for Shipman. Family members testified that their loved one had never used morphine, even though Shipman had written a prescription in their name.

"He was addicted to death. He got a thrill out of seeing people die."[5]

—Denis Maher, a priest in Hyde who knew several of Shipman's victims

In police interviews, Shipman had insisted that he had not kept morphine at his home or office since his drug addiction years earlier. However, the prosecution revealed that the police had found a bag at the Shipman home containing a stash of morphine and vials of diamorphine that Shipman had prescribed in the name of several patients.

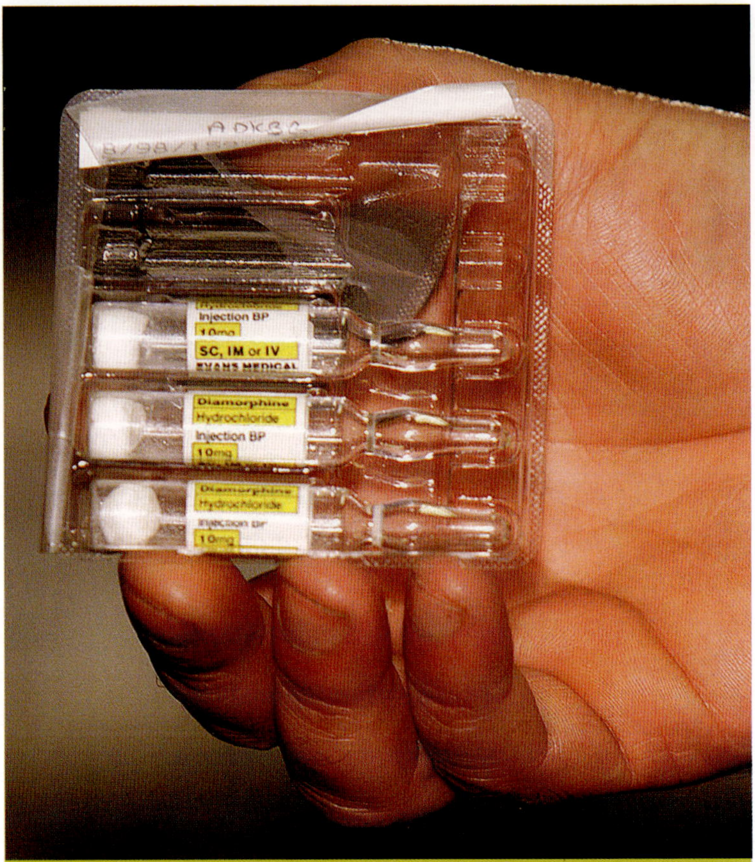

During a search of Shipman's house, police collected morphine from an upstairs bedroom. However, the evidence was not examined closely and was discovered only weeks before the trial.

The Defense Responds

The defense team was led by Nicola Davies, a lawyer who specialized in medical cases. She had been asked to join the case by Anne Ball, Shipman's original lawyer. As witnesses testified for the prosecution, the defense cross-examined them but did little to cast doubt on their testimony.

On November 25, the defense's case began. Shipman took the stand to testify. In a low, quiet voice, he gave details about his training and career. He described his usual routine at his medical office and how he cared for his patients. As Shipman spoke, his wife and one of his sons watched from the gallery.

As Shipman's testimony continued, he became more comfortable, occasionally offering glimpses of his arrogant attitude. When asked about Kathleen Grundy's death, Shipman explained that he believed she was taking drugs that she had gotten from someone else. "I didn't talk to anybody else about it like a colleague or consultant. I was just being suspicious. I thought she was abusing a drug—it had to be something like an opiate, codeine, pethidine, or perhaps morphine," he said.[6] When Davies asked him directly if he had killed Grundy, Shipman replied with a forceful, "No, I did not."[7]

Shipman denied forging Grundy's will. He explained that she had borrowed his typewriter a few times. Shipman insisted that he had never seen the forged will until the police showed it to him. When asked how his fingerprint got on the will, Shipman explained he must have touched it when Grundy asked him to witness the signature in his office.

Over the next few days on the witness stand, Shipman spoke about the medical treatment of each patient he was accused of killing. Throughout his testimony, Shipman insisted that the women died of natural causes. He admitted to backdating computer entries but explained that he was ensuring his files were complete and accurate. He emphasized that he did not kill any of his patients.

"You never suspect a doctor of doing anything other but to help a patient's health."[8]

–Brian Dean, son of Shipman victim Joan Dean

During the prosecution's cross-examination, Shipman appeared uncomfortable. For seven days, Henriques pointed out inconsistencies in Shipman's medical records and the similarities in each death. Shipman was not able to explain why morphine was found in the exhumed bodies of the victims, though he at one point suggested that Grundy may have been abusing drugs.

After Shipman's cross-examination, the defense called only one other witness, a fingerprint expert who talked about the prints found on Grundy's will. The defense did not call any toxicology experts to dispute the prosecution's morphine findings. By mid-December, the defense had finished.

With cameras highly restricted in the courtroom, court illustrations gave people a window into unaired parts of Shipman's trial.

Closing Statements

In January 2000, the prosecution and defense presented closing statements to the jury. Henriques addressed the jury first. He reminded them about the evidence they had heard from more than 120 prosecution witnesses. Henriques told the jury that Shipman had betrayed the trust his patients and their families had given him and tricked them to hide his murders.

"He took advantage of their grief and their lesser knowledge of medicine and procedures. As they grieved, this determined man employed every device to make sure no post-mortem examination took place," said Henriques.[9] In all 15 cases, Henriques pointed out that Shipman had not called an ambulance or attempted to resuscitate the women because he already knew they were dead.

During Shipman's trial, seats were reserved for Primrose and their children in the court's gallery.

When it was time for the defense to give their closing statement, Davies took the floor. She told the jury that there was no motive for Shipman to kill his patients. She described Shipman as a caring doctor who would do anything for his patients. Davies explained away any discrepancies in Shipman's medical records as simply the result of a doctor prioritizing patient care over paperwork.

Davies also questioned the prosecution's toxicology evidence and insisted it was unreliable. "The prosecution case is built on one foundation stone and that is toxicology," Davies said. "Without it there would be no case. Toxicology is a new science and untested by proven scientific methods."[10]

Verdict and Sentencing

After the lawyers finished their closing arguments, the judge spoke to the jury. He summed up the trial and instructed the jury to put away their emotions during deliberations. The judge also told the jury that they must not consider anything they had seen or heard about the case outside the courtroom in their decision.

On January 24, the jury began deliberating. In the late afternoon of January 31, the jury returned with a verdict. They found Shipman guilty on all 15 counts of murder and

THE 15 VICTIMS

Shipman was found guilty of murdering 15 women:

- Lizzie Adams, 77
- Muriel Grimshaw, 76
- Kathleen Grundy, 81
- Pamela Hillier, 68
- Jean Lilley, 58
- Ivy Lomas, 63
- Joan Melia, 73
- Winifred Mellor, 73
- Norah Nuttall, 65
- Bianka Pomfret, 49
- Marie Quinn, 67
- Irene Turner, 67
- Laura Kathleen Wagstaff, 81
- Maureen Ward, 57
- Marie West, 81

one count of forgery. As the verdicts were read, Shipman showed no emotion. Wearing black in the gallery, Primrose remained emotionless, while two of her sons lowered their eyes.

The court moved on to the sentencing process. The prosecution asked the judge to take Shipman's previous drug convictions into account, a fact that had not been allowed during the trial. The prosecution explained Shipman's history of obtaining drugs illegally, eliciting a gasp from people in the public viewing area.

Davies asked the judge to sentence Shipman immediately. The judge agreed, asked Shipman to stand, and spoke directly to him. "You have finally been brought to justice by the verdicts of this jury," the judge announced. "I have no doubt whatsoever but that these are true verdicts. The time has now come for me to pass sentence upon you for these wicked, wicked crimes."[11] The judge sentenced Shipman to prison for 15 life sentences, one for each murder, and four additional years for forgery.[12]

After the verdict, Grundy's daughter, Angela Woodruff, stood on the steps of the court. She struggled to control her emotions as she spoke to the media. "We are pleased that the trial is over and relieved at the outcome," Woodruff said. "It's just awful the way that he abused the trust which all his patients had in him. It's evil. [My mother] would tell us about him, how caring he was. The betrayal is one of the things that I really find it hard to come to terms with; that the doctor that you respected and you thought respected you had betrayed you."[13]

The trial of Harold Shipman was finally over. The families of the 15 victims had some form of closure for their loved ones. However, the true magnitude of Shipman's crimes was yet to be discovered.

STATEMENT FROM VICTIM'S FAMILY

On December 9, 1997, Shipman injected 81-year-old Laura Kathleen Wagstaff with a fatal dose of morphine. For months, her family believed Shipman when he claimed Wagstaff had died of heart disease. However, when Shipman was found guilty of Wagstaff's murder, the family issued a statement. They said, "We feel a sense of relief that this part of the nightmare is at an end and justice has been done. To lose our mother in such circumstances leaves us with a feeling of deep sadness that we were so badly betrayed by someone in whom we had great trust."[14]

CHAPTER 9

SHIPMAN'S DEATH AND LEGACY

After the verdict, Shipman was sent to Frankland Prison, a maximum-security prison near Durham, England. The prison housed high-risk offenders who were serving sentences longer than four years. Inside, Shipman's fellow inmates included drug dealers, armed robbers, violent thieves, and a few like him who were serving life sentences.

Life in Prison

At Frankland, Shipman soon fell into a routine. He read the newspaper during breakfast before spending some time reading and replying to letters. Shipman had a television in his cell, which he used to watch sports and game shows. He wore pants and sweaters as the prison did not require inmates to wear a prison uniform. He also used the prison gym regularly. His main complaint was that the prison was cold.

Today, the Garden of Tranquility in Hyde, England, honors the victims of Harold Shipman.

At Frankland, Shipman caused little trouble for the prison staff. However, he could be condescending at times and wanted to be called Dr. Shipman instead of Fred. He also was not always compliant. Inmates were encouraged to participate in therapy and show remorse for their crimes, but Shipman was not interested in therapy. He refused to talk about his crimes or see a psychiatrist.

While Shipman adjusted to prison, Primrose adjusted to living without her husband. She sold the family home in Hyde and by 2001 had bought a small cottage near her

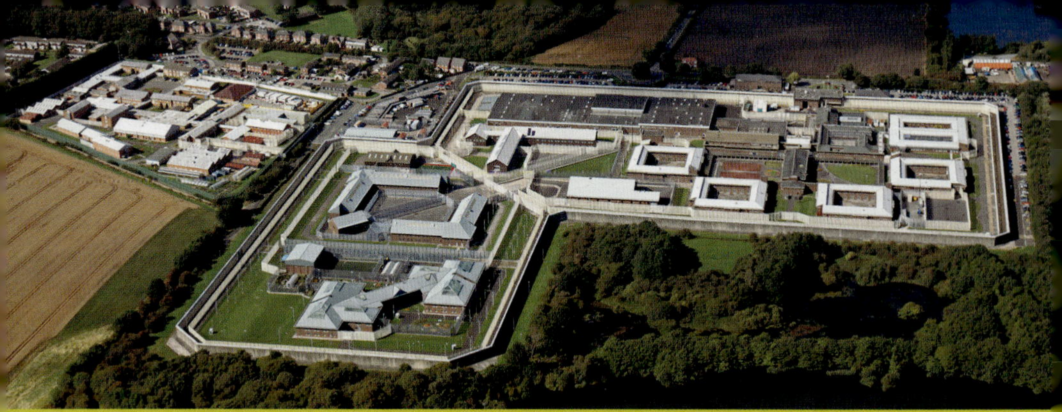

Frankland Prison holds some of the most dangerous criminals in the United Kingdom.

childhood hometown of Wetherby. Primrose regularly visited Shipman. Sometimes, one of their sons went with her. At each visit, the couple held hands.

At Frankland, prisoners with medical conditions regularly asked Shipman for advice. He occasionally assisted disabled prisoners, pushing wheelchairs and helping elderly inmates into bed. However, when the public learned that Shipman was caring for the ill and elderly, they admonished prison officials for allowing Shipman to play the role of doctor. After initially denying the charges, the prison admitted that the accusations were true. Experts warned that Shipman should be banned from contact with the ill and elderly; they believed that, given the opportunity, Shipman would kill again.

The Final Death

In June 2003, Shipman was moved from Frankland to Wakefield Prison. Officials described the move as routine, placing him closer to Primrose in Wetherby. However, Wakefield was an old prison that held many murderers serving life sentences, and the conditions were much more restrictive.

At Wakefield, Shipman spent 14 to 20 hours locked in his cell every day. He was allowed only two visits per month from Primrose. Prison officials were also less tolerant of Shipman's attitude and refusal to attend therapy. He lost multiple privileges, such as the right to wear his personal clothing and have a television in his cell.

PLANNED APPEAL

At the time of his death, Shipman was planning to appeal his 15 murder convictions. The appeal claimed that Shipman's defense lawyers should have been allowed to have their own autopsies carried out on 11 victims.[1] When Shipman was found dead, plans for the appeal were canceled.

On January 13, 2004, Wakefield prison officials found Shipman dead in his cell. He had hanged himself with a noose made from bedsheets. Officials were unable to revive him.

Many relatives of Shipman's victims were angry when they learned of the doctor's suicide. In their view, he had managed to escape his punishment through death. "Hanging was too good for Shipman," said Brian Dean, whose mother, Joan Dean, was killed by Shipman

The day before Shipman died by suicide, he had a phone call with his wife. Primrose says she was unaware that Shipman was planning to end his life.

in 1998. "He had been trapped like a bird in a gilded cage, knowing that he would never be free, and that was fine with me. He took the easy way out."[2]

Many had hoped Shipman would eventually explain why he murdered their loved ones. Now, they would never get that answer. Ann Alexander, a lawyer who represented many relatives of the victims, described her clients' emotions upon hearing of Shipman's death:

"Many of the relatives had hoped that one day Harold Shipman would have answered many of the questions that they have surrounding their relative's death, in particular why he committed these terrible crimes. He has never shown any remorse, and the families with whom we have spoken . . . are extremely distressed at this news."[3]

ONE LAST GIFT FOR PRIMROSE

Some people have speculated that 57-year-old Shipman timed his suicide to provide for his wife, Primrose. Upon Shipman's death, Primrose received a lump-sum payment and an annual pension of more than 100,000 British pounds, the equivalent of $222,000 in today's currency.[4] If Shipman had lived to age 60, Primrose would have received a significantly smaller pension and no lump-sum payment. A probation officer reported that Shipman had talked to him about the plan. Despite the conversation being reported to prison officials, Shipman was not put on suicide watch.

The Shipman Inquiry

The Shipman case left many wondering how a doctor had been able to get away with murdering his patients for so long. Although Shipman had been convicted of only 15 murders, many people believed that his true death count was higher. Some suspected that his killings had started long before he began practicing in Hyde.

In February 2000, Secretary of State for Health Alan Milburn announced there would be an independent public inquiry into the Shipman case. Janet Smith, a High Court judge, was selected to lead the inquiry. The inquiry would investigate the extent of Shipman's crimes, review why they had not been detected earlier, and determine how similar crimes could be prevented in the future. In June 2001, public hearings began in the Manchester town hall.

The Shipman Inquiry produced six reports between 2002 and 2005. The first report, published in 2002, found that Shipman had murdered 215 patients, making him England's most prolific serial killer. The report also noted that more than 200 additional patient deaths were highly suspicious. Of the 215 victims, 171 were women and 44 were men. They ranged in age from a 47-year-old man to a 93-year-old woman. The findings were based on police and medical records and testimony from relatives. After the report was released, church bells in Hyde rang 215 times in memory of the victims.[5]

Subsequent inquiry reports criticized the earlier police investigations that failed to recognize Shipman's crimes. "If the police and the coroner had moved with reasonable expedition, the lives of Shipman's last three victims would probably have been saved," Smith said.[6] The inquiry called for reforms in how coroners investigated deaths and issued death certificates. By issuing death certificates that stated natural causes, Shipman had been able to escape investigation. The inquiry also called for measures to prevent doctors from stockpiling dangerous drugs.

The inquiry's final report, published in January 2005, increased the number of Shipman victims to a staggering 250 and concluded that he may have begun killing within a year of finishing medical school. "In many cases, I have been unable to reach a definite conclusion," said Smith. "With this sixth report, I believe that the Inquiry has finally provided as complete a picture of Shipman's activity as it would be possible to give."[7]

EVA LYONS

The Shipman Inquiry named 71-year-old Eva Lyons as Shipman's first known victim. The cancer patient died in 1975 after a late-night house call in Todmorden from Shipman. He injected Lyons with a fatal dose of diamorphine and then asked her husband, Richard, for a cup of coffee. A few minutes later, Shipman informed Richard that Lyons was dead. Twenty-five years after her death, the Lyons family learned Eva had been murdered. Today, the family believes more Shipman victims have not yet been identified.

Changes in the Medical Community

One of the key recommendations from the Shipman Inquiry was that a second independent medical professional should examine every death. In 2009, the

United Kingdom passed legislation to establish a new system of medical examiners to review any death that did not involve a coroner. However, no date was set for it to begin. As a result, hospitals did not start introducing the new roles until 2019.

"[Shipman's] motive was power over life and death. He was like Dracula, after blood."[9]

—Constance O'Neil, daughter of Shipman victim Alice Gorton

Meanwhile, some doctors made voluntary changes to their procedures. In Hyde, Raj Patel worked with colleagues to create new procedures so that a second doctor could contact relatives with any questions about cremation forms. Patel persuaded doctors throughout Manchester to adopt the revised procedures. By 2008, the new procedures were standard practice across the United Kingdom.

"It was really important because we knew there were gaps in the system to allow Shipman to get away with what he did," Patel said, "and what we were waiting for was some national guidance that wasn't coming, so we decided locally as doctors that we would make some changes and these changes were adopted."[8] Patel also helped to create a controlled drugs incident report tool that has since been adopted across most of England.

Motive Remains Unknown

While the inquiry into Harold Shipman prompted important changes in how deaths are handled, for 250 patients, these changes came too late. Families of victims struggled to find closure. Despite the extensive reports about Shipman's crimes, little is known about the doctor's motives. Ultimately, Shipman never admitted guilt or explained his actions.

Some have suggested that he was recreating the death of his mother, Vera, while others believe he was practicing euthanasia or mercy killings of the old and sick. Many believe that Shipman was a man who simply relished having the power of life and death in his hands. As for Detective Superintendent Bernard Postles, he still has no answer to the frequent questions he receives asking why Shipman committed so many heinous crimes. "We don't seem to be able to identify a motive," he says. "Beyond that we are into speculation."[10]

"I think the nearest I can get to explaining what motivated him was that I think that he felt he knew best when it was time for somebody to die. I suppose in a way it made him compare himself to God."[11]

—Janet Smith, head of the Shipman Inquiry

ESSENTIAL FACTS

TIMELINE

Jan. 14, 1946: Harold Frederick Shipman is born in Nottingham, England, to Vera and Harold Shipman.

1965: Shipman begins studying medicine at the University of Leeds and meets Primrose Oxtoby.

1974: Shipman joins a general medical practice in Todmorden, England. Within a year, Shipman's addiction to pethidine is revealed and he is forced to leave Todmorden.

1977: Shipman joins the Donneybrook medical practice in Hyde, England.

June 1998: Kathleen Grundy dies after a house call from Shipman, and a suspicious will leaves her estate to Shipman. Grundy's daughter goes to the police with concerns that the will is a forgery.

Aug. 1998: Investigators exhume Grundy's body. Forensic testing reveals that Grundy was killed by a lethal dose of morphine.

Sept.–Dec. 1998: Police arrest Shipman for the murder of Grundy and forgery of her will. In the meantime, additional bodies are exhumed in Hyde and more charges are brought against Shipman.

1999–2000: Harold Shipman is found guilty of 15 counts of murder and sentenced to life in prison.

2002–2005: The Shipman Inquiry investigates the extent of Shipman's crimes and how they could have been prevented. The inquiry produces six reports, finally concluding that Shipman murdered at least 250 patients.

Jan. 13, 2004: Shipman dies by suicide in prison.

IMPACT ON SOCIETY

Harold Shipman was a trusted doctor for thousands of patients, caring for them in their most vulnerable moments. He betrayed the trust of his patients, their families, and the community by murdering 250 patients over the span of two decades. He covered up his crimes by signing death certificates that attributed his patients' deaths to natural causes. He falsified medical records and encouraged families to cremate the bodies of his victims to get rid of the evidence.

The Shipman case had a lasting impact on medicine in the United Kingdom. The public inquiry into the case, the Shipman Inquiry, revealed several shortcomings in the way the police and the medical community report and investigate deaths. The inquiry called for reforms in several processes, including how coroners investigate deaths and issue death certificates. It also identified reforms that were needed for the handling of certain drugs. The lessons learned from the Shipman case may help prevent similar crimes from happening in the future.

QUOTE

"The defendant killed those 15 patients because, in the submission of the prosecution, he enjoyed doing so. He was exercising the ultimate power of controlling life and death and repeated the act so often he must have found the drama of taking life to his taste."

—Richard Henriques, lead prosecution attorney, in his opening statement at the Shipman trial

GLOSSARY

appeal

A legal proceeding submitted to ask a higher court to review the decision of a lower court.

autopsy

An examination of a dead body to determine the cause of death.

cremation

The disposal of a body by burning it to ashes.

emaciated

Extremely thin and weak, usually because of hunger or illness.

exhume

To remove a body from the ground.

forensic pathologist

An expert in determining a person's cause and manner of death.

forgery

An unauthorized copy of a document, a signature, money, or a work of art.

general practitioner (GP)

A medical doctor who is trained to provide primary health care and does not specialize in an area of expertise.

hospice care

Care for dying patients to make them more comfortable in their final days.

modus operandi

A method of doing something, especially committing a crime.

prosecution

The legal party that leads the case against a defendant in court.

psychologist

A person who specializes in the study of the mind.

terminal

Fatal.

toxicologist

A scientist who typically works with chemicals and other substances to determine if they are harmful.

toxins

Naturally occurring poisons.

undertaker

A person who prepares for and manages funerals and burials.

ADDITIONAL RESOURCES

SELECTED BIBLIOGRAPHY

Coyle, Simon. "Who Were the Victims of Harold Shipman and How Many Murders Was He Convicted Of?" *Manchester Evening News*, 26 Apr. 2018, manchestereveningnews.co.uk. Accessed 18 Apr. 2024.

Eichenwald, Kurt. "Deadly House Calls: A Special Report.; True English Murder Mystery: Town's Trusted Doctor Did It." *New York Times*, 13 May 2001, nytimes.com. Accessed 10 Apr. 2024.

Whittle, Brian, and Jean Ritchie. *Prescription for Murder: The True Story of Mass Murderer Dr. Harold Frederick Shipman*. Warner, 2000.

FURTHER READINGS

Cooper, Christopher. *Forensic Science*. DK, 2020.

Morris, Rebecca. *Joseph James DeAngelo: The Golden State Killer*. Abdo, 2025.

Newquist, H. P. *Scene of the Crime: Tracking Down Criminals with Forensic Science*. Viking, 2021.

ONLINE RESOURCES

Booklinks
NONFICTION NETWORK
FREE! ONLINE NONFICTION RESOURCES

To learn more about serial killers, please visit **abdobooklinks.com** or scan this QR code. These links are routinely monitored and updated to provide the most current information available.

MORE INFORMATION

For more information on this subject, contact or visit the following organizations:

ALCATRAZ EAST CRIME MUSEUM

2757 Pkwy.
Pigeon Forge, TN 37863
alcatrazeast.com

The Alcatraz East Crime Museum provides information about crime scene investigation and famous cases.

AMERICAN ACADEMY OF FORENSIC SCIENCES (AAFS)

410 N. 21st St.
Colorado Springs, CO 80904
aafs.org

The AAFS is a professional society dedicated to promoting forensic science education and improving accuracy and precision in forensic science.

GENERAL MEDICAL COUNCIL

350 Euston Rd.
London, United Kingdom NW1 3AW
gmc-uk.org

The General Medical Council is a public organization that registers and regulates doctors and other medical practitioners in the United Kingdom.

SOURCE NOTES

CHAPTER 1. UNEARTHING A MURDER

1. "Kathleen's Exhumation a First for Police." *Manchester Evening News*, 3 Oct. 2007, manchestereveningnews.co.uk. Accessed 21 June 2024.

2. Brian Whittle and Jean Ritchie. *Prescription for Murder: The True Story of Mass Murderer Dr. Harold Frederick Shipman*. Warner, 2000. 15–16.

3. Whittle and Ritchie, *Prescription for Murder*, 1.

4. David Ward. "'Last Victim' Welcomed Home Visit by Shipman." *Guardian*, 14 Oct. 1999, theguardian.com. Accessed 21 June 2024.

5. Kurt Eichenwald. "Deadly House Calls: A Special Report.; True English Murder Mystery: Town's Trusted Doctor Did It." *New York Times*, 13 May 2001, nytimes.com. Accessed 21 June 2024.

6. Andrew Walker. "Newsmaker: Angela Woodruff." *BBC News*, 4 Feb. 2000, news.bbc.co.uk. Accessed 21 June 2024.

CHAPTER 2. CHILDHOOD AND EARLY INFLUENCES

1. Brian Whittle and Jean Ritchie. *Prescription for Murder: The True Story of Mass Murderer Dr. Harold Frederick Shipman*. Warner, 2000. 30.

2. Whittle and Ritchie, *Prescription for Murder*, 33.

3. Whittle and Ritchie, *Prescription for Murder*, 39.

4. Whittle and Ritchie, *Prescription for Murder*, 40.

5. Whittle and Ritchie, *Prescription for Murder*, 44.

CHAPTER 3. INTEREST IN MEDICINE

1. Brian Whittle and Jean Ritchie. *Prescription for Murder: The True Story of Mass Murderer Dr. Harold Frederick Shipman*. Warner, 2000. 75–76.

2. Whittle and Ritchie, *Prescription for Murder*, 85–86.

3. Whittle and Ritchie, *Prescription for Murder*, 86.

4. Michael Newton. *The Encyclopedia of Serial Killers*. Facts On File, 2006. 239.

5. "The Man Who Played God." *BBC News*, 1 Jan. 2000, news.bbc.co.uk. Accessed 21 June 2024.

6. Whittle and Ritchie, *Prescription for Murder*, 96.

CHAPTER 4. A TRUSTED DOCTOR

1. Nigel Bunyan. "The Killing Fields of Harold Shipman." *Telegraph*, 16 June 2001, telegraph.co.uk. Accessed 21 June 2024.

2. Brian Whittle and Jean Ritchie. *Prescription for Murder: The True Story of Mass Murderer Dr. Harold Frederick Shipman*. Warner, 2000. 106.

3. Whittle and Ritchie, *Prescription for Murder*, 112.

4. Whittle and Ritchie, *Prescription for Murder*, 113–114.
5. David Ward and Helen Carter. "The Doctor Jekyll of Hyde." *Guardian*, 31 Jan. 2000, theguardian.com. Accessed 21 June 2024.
6. Whittle and Ritchie, *Prescription for Murder*, 142–143.
7. Whittle and Ritchie, *Prescription for Murder*, 144.

CHAPTER 5. FIRST SUSPICIONS

1. Marjorie Miller. "The Doctor Who Killed Old Ladies." *Los Angeles Times*, 6 Jan. 2001, latimes.com. Accessed 21 June 2024.
2. Brian Whittle and Jean Ritchie. *Prescription for Murder: The True Story of Mass Murderer Dr. Harold Frederick Shipman*. Warner, 2000. 169.
3. Kurt Eichenwald. "Deadly House Calls: A Special Report.; True English Murder Mystery: Town's Trusted Doctor Did It." *New York Times*, 13 May 2001, nytimes.com. Accessed 21 June 2024.
4. Eichenwald, "Deadly House Calls."
5. Eichenwald, "Deadly House Calls."
6. David Ward and Helen Carter. "Free to Kill Again after Earlier Inquiry Halted." *Guardian*, 31 Jan. 2000, theguardian.com. Accessed 21 June 2024.
7. Dame Janet Smith. *The Shipman Inquiry: Second Report: The Police Investigation of March 1998*. The Stationery Office, 2003. 5.

CHAPTER 6. DEATH AND FORGERY

1. Brian Hurwitz. "Murder Most Medical, Disposal Most Discreet." *Lancet*, Dec. 2004, thelancet.com. Accessed 21 June 2024.
2. David Ward and Helen Carter. "Typewriter Trail That Unmasked a Careful Killer." *Guardian*, 31 Jan. 2000, theguardian.com. Accessed 21 June 2024.
3. "The Death That Led Shipman to the Dock." *BBC News*, 31 Jan. 2000, news.bbc.co.uk. Accessed 21 June 2024.
4. Helen Carter. "Daughter 'Could Not Believe' Will in GP's Favor." *Guardian*, 14 Oct. 1999, theguardian.com. Accessed 21 June 2024.
5. Kurt Eichenwald. "Deadly House Calls: A Special Report.; True English Murder Mystery: Town's Trusted Doctor Did It." *New York Times*, 13 May 2001, nytimes.com. Accessed 21 June 2024.
6. Carter, "Daughter 'Could Not Believe' Will in GP's Favor."
7. Brian Whittle and Jean Ritchie. *Prescription for Murder: The True Story of Mass Murderer Dr. Harold Frederick Shipman*. Warner, 2000. 19.
8. "Shipman's Stolen Gems Found in His Wife's Jewelry Box." *Guardian*, 31 Aug. 2005, theguardian.com. Accessed 21 June 2024.
9. Eichenwald, "Deadly House Calls."

SOURCE NOTES CONTINUED

10. "Police Story: Investigating Shipman." *BBC News*, 31 Jan. 2000, news.bbc.co.uk. Accessed 21 June 2024.

11. Whittle and Ritchie, *Prescription for Murder*, 186.

12. Whittle and Ritchie, *Prescription for Murder*, 186.

CHAPTER 7. EXHUMATIONS AND ARREST

1. Brian Whittle and Jean Ritchie. *Prescription for Murder: The True Story of Mass Murderer Dr. Harold Frederick Shipman*. Warner, 2000. 198.

2. David Ward and Helen Carter. "Typewriter Trail That Unmasked a Careful Killer." *Guardian*, 31 Jan. 2000, theguardian.com. Accessed 21 June 2024.

3. Ward and Carter, "Typewriter Trail."

4. Ward and Carter, "Typewriter Trail."

5. "Police Interview: Winifred Mellor." *Guardian*, 31 Jan. 2000, theguardian.com. Accessed 21 June 2024.

6. "Harold Shipman: A Chronology." *Guardian*, 25 Aug. 2005, theguardian.com. Accessed 21 June 2024.

7. Marjorie Miller. "The Doctor Who Killed Old Ladies." *Los Angeles Times*, 6 Jan. 2001, latimes.com. Accessed 21 June 2024.

8. Whittle and Ritchie, *Prescription for Murder*, 242.

9. David Ward and Helen Carter. "Trial of GP Charged with Murder of 15 Patients Adjourned." *Guardian*, 6 Oct. 1999, theguardian.com. Accessed 21 June 2024.

CHAPTER 8. THE TRIAL BEGINS

1. David Ward and Helen Carter. "Trial of GP Charged with Murder of 15 Patients Adjourned." *Guardian*, 6 Oct. 1999, theguardian.com. Accessed 21 June 2024.

2. Brian Whittle and Jean Ritchie. *Prescription for Murder: The True Story of Mass Murderer Dr. Harold Frederick Shipman*. Warner, 2000. 296.

3. David Ward. "Doctor 'Killed 15 for Pleasure and Power.'" *Guardian*, 12 Oct. 1999, theguardian.com. Accessed 21 June 2024.

4. Ward, "Doctor 'Killed 15 for Pleasure and Power.'"

5. Marjorie Miller. "The Doctor Who Killed Old Ladies." *Los Angeles Times*, 6 Jan. 2001, latimes.com. Accessed 21 June 2024.

6. Helen Carter and David Ward. "Shipman: I Did Not Kill 15 Patients." *Guardian*, 25 Nov. 1999, theguardian.com. Accessed 21 June 2024.

7. Whittle and Ritchie, *Prescription for Murder*, 303.

8. Jamie Wilson and Vikram Dodd. "Victims' Families Speak of Grief." *Guardian*, 31 Jan. 2000, theguardian.com. Accessed 21 June 2024.

9. Ros Taylor. "Deaths No Coincidence, Shipman Trial Told." *Guardian*, 5 Jan. 2000, theguardian.com. Accessed 21 June 2024.

10. Helen Carter. "Case against Doctor Is Unreliable, Says QC." *Guardian*, 6 Jan. 2000, theguardian.com. Accessed 21 June 2024.

11. "Take Him Down." *Manchester Evening News*, 3 Oct. 2007, manchestereveningnews.co.uk. Accessed 21 June 2024.

12. Wilson and Dodd, "Victims' Families Speak of Grief."

13. Wilson and Dodd, "Victims' Families Speak of Grief."

14. Wilson and Dodd, "Victims' Families Speak of Grief."

CHAPTER 9. SHIPMAN'S DEATH AND LEGACY

1. "Families' Fury over Shipman Bid to Appeal." *Manchester Evening News*, 10 Aug. 2004, manchestereveningnews.co.uk. Accessed 21 June 2024.

2. "'He Has Controlled Us All the Way . . . He Has Controlled the Last Step and I Hate Him for It'; The Relatives of Serial Killer's Victims Express Their Outrage." *Herald*, 13 Jan. 2004, heraldscotland.com. Accessed 21 June 2024.

3. "'He Has Controlled Us All the Way.'"

4. Mark Oliver. "Shipman Died 'to Ensure Wife's Pension.'" *Guardian*, 15 Jan. 2004, theguardian.com. Accessed 21 June 2024.

5. "Shipman 'Killed 215 Patients.'" *BBC News*, 20 July 2002, news.bbc.co.uk. Accessed 21 June 2024.

6. "At-a-Glance: The Shipman Reports." *BBC News*, 27 Jan. 2005, news.bbc.co.uk. Accessed 21 June 2024.

7. "Shipman 'Killed Early in Career.'" *BBC News*, 27 Jan. 2005, news.bbc.co.uk. Accessed 21 June 2024.

8. "Queens Birthday Honours 2019: MBE for Doctor Who Led Post-Shipman Reforms." *BBC News*, 7 June 2019, news.bbc.co.uk. Accessed 21 June 2024.

9. "Police Story: Investigating Shipman." *BBC News*, 31 Jan. 2000, news.bbc.co.uk. Accessed 21 June 2024.

10. "British Doctor May Have Killed 600." *ABC News*, 20 June 2001, abcnews.go.com. Accessed 21 June 2024.

11. "Shipman Letters Reveal Killer 'Thought He Was a God'." *BBC News*, 19 July 2010, news.bbc.co.uk. Accessed 21 June 2024.

INDEX

ABOUT THE AUTHOR

CARLA MOONEY

Carla Mooney is a graduate of the University of Pennsylvania. Today, she writes for young people and is the author of many books for young adults and children. Mooney enjoys reading about true crime and investigations.